The 3 Step Structured Approach to Managing your Credit & Finances®

Library of Congress Cataloging-in-Publication Data

ISBN: 978-1-953994-02-8

Printed in the United States of America

Self-Published

Text design by Thomas (TJ) Underwood

The 3 Step Structured Approach to Managing your Credit & Finances®

A Powerful Guide That Will Help You Attain the Financial Success That You Desire

The "3 Step Structured Approach" provides you the most cost-effective, time-efficient and easier to learn and apply system of comprehensively managing your credit and finances that can be found in personal finance and is now available for purchase for less than $10.00! The "3 Step Structured Approach" will provide you a mental system of managing your credit and finances (that you can carry within your mind and apply effectively) for the rest of your life.

The "3 Step Structured Approach" will provide you the blueprint of what you need to do to improve your cash flow, manage your credit and address all areas of your finances from a comprehensive perspective—thereby significantly increasing the odds that you will attain your future goals. Updated in 2023 to provide you even more insight so that you can achieve more in the coming years.

Why You Must Properly Focus on Your Goals

It is important that you learn how you can use "the power of focus" to direct your and your family's future. Likewise, it is important that you see your financial future from a better perspective.

Proper preparation on your part will go a long way in giving you the "proper focus" that is needed for your and your family's future credit and finance success.

By comprehending the following paragraphs at your highest level—you can learn how to improve your focus daily—so that you can attain the goals that will serve your and your family's best long-term interests!

If you see your credit and financial future clearly and you focus on what is truly important by utilizing the empowering credit and finance information and advice in this book—you can reach your goals and objectives in not only an effective manner—but also a more efficient manner.

Proper focus allows you to concentrate on what is truly important and will take you and your family to where you need or want to be!

If your goal is to manage and improve your credit and finances to a high level, you can do so if you have the right focus.

Having the right focus means concentrating on your future goals and objectives with laser like precision.

By having the know-how of what you need to do—and actually knowing how you can improve your credit and finances to a high level—you can put yourself in position for major success in your and your family's future.

If you use your know-how, proper execution and **proper focus**, all working in conjunction—you make your and your family's future success much more likely to occur.

It is also important that you include written goal setting as part of your focusing efforts—if you truly want to reach your and your family's future goals.

Focusing allows you to make room in your mind to put what you really want to "achieve" at the forefront of your mental thought process on a daily basis.

"Proper focus" requires that you block out all negative distractions in your life and not let the opinions of others deter you from reaching your goals.

*Did you know that there are **basically 3 ways** that you can approach occurrences that will happen in your life or that may happen around you?*

1) there are things in life that you absolutely cannot change

2) there are things in life that you could possibly change—but you are often reluctant to do so for varying reasons

3) there are things that are **totally under your control**—and you have the power to do something about in a meaningful and significant way—today

The **3rd option** mentioned above is what this E-book focuses on and it is what you too should spend your energy focusing on—if you desire to maximize your future success!

You must focus on things that you can do something about—RIGHT NOW—at this time!

By "consciously or unconsciously" focusing on the **1st or 2nd option** above by complaining, making excuses and otherwise letting distractions rule over you—on a consistent basis—you are displaying a lack of understanding of how to truly transform your future and by doing so you are taking your focus in a direction that does not best serve your long-term interests!

Because you can't or often won't do anything about what you can't change or possibly change—you are wasting mental energy that you could be using to focus on things that you can change—and things that you absolutely have the power to change!

By properly focusing and using written goals, you give your mind even more clarity and your daily mindset will be improved because you will know with certainty that if you focus and do what you put in writing—your future goals will be attained!

Don't let your dreams, thoughts and goals die inside of your mind! Put them in writing—and then take action and "properly focus" to make what you desire a reality!

Did you know that some of your most powerful thoughts and ideas (inside your mind) will float away and possibly never return, if you don't put them in writing or record your thoughts and ideas in some other manner?

By putting your thoughts, ideas and goals in writing you can improve your focus and reach your and your family's credit and financial goals!

Proper Focus means that you are paying attention to your future goals at such a high level that you see your success clearly and you know in your mind and heart that you will not be distracted along the way!

You know with a high level of certainty that you are "truly serious" and you intend on reaching your future goals in an efficient and effective manner!

Proper focus is a quality that you must have if your goal is to attain your goals and objectives in an efficient manner.

If you sincerely want success for yourself and your family—you must focus on reaching your goals at your highest level.

Doing so will put you on a path to true success. Once you focus and attain your goals on a consistent basis you will be in position to enjoy your life on your terms. You will no longer be at a disadvantage in your credit and financial life.

You must have a yearning, passion, and true desire to reach your goals—whatever they may be!

If you are "properly focused" and you have a "true desire" to reach your credit and financial goals—others will feel and see your enthusiasm and your future success will be more likely to occur.

Likewise, if you are not properly focused and you are not truly determined to reach your credit and financial goals—your future success will be less likely to occur.

It is important that you focus your thoughts on what you desire and likewise you must desire what you focus on!

There is no reason why you should focus on (waste energy)—whether consciously or unconsciously—things that you can't do anything about or things that you won't do anything about—if you desire to attain success in a more effective and efficient manner!

Remember, to be highly successful you must "properly focus" and you must have "passion" in whatever you do! You must not pursue your goals half-heartedly!

Use the knowledge that you have just learned to your and your family's best advantage!

Proper preparation and proper focus—along with a burning desire to succeed on the inside along with a high level of determination—will take your success to a high level.

Do you have "staying power" when things get tough? The way you look at life and how you respond to adversity is the key to your and your family's future success!

You must be "unstoppable" in your journey toward reaching your goals and objectives. No obstacle or adversity that you encounter should detour (or deter) you from reaching your and your family's future credit and financial goals!

You must always focus on what you want to bring into existence—and you must bring into existence that which you want by properly focusing on what you desire!

You cannot merely talk about what you desire, think about what you desire or dream about what you desire. To truly reach your goals you must take action and make what you desire a reality!

When you really get down to it—execution is all that really counts!

You must also find out what you are passionate about and what your true calling or gift in your life really is!

You must not do like many who live their life inappropriately and when they reach their golden years they look back in regret—after knowing that they had the gift to do more.

You must realize that you now have the potential to achieve many of your credit and financial goals by reading this book—however, potential to do so is really nothing!

Until you sincerely decide to put into action that which can really benefit you and your family on a consistent basis—potential serves no real purpose!

You can change the patterns of your past and do more in your life! You can change your future for the better in a major way—starting today!

This E-book provides you a "real opportunity" to recalibrate your mind and provides you the opportunity to master the **mental working knowledge** that you need to succeed—**BIG TIME!**

What do you really desire at this time?

You must now find out what you really desire in your future **and properly focus** and prepare your mind to make it happen!

The **"3 Step Approach"** and the **other structuring methods** that you will soon learn will provided you the clarity and focus that you need—to succeed!

You will soon have a clear and unambiguous understanding of what you need to do to make what you desire a reality, and you will now soon have the blueprint for a lifetime of success—wrapped inside of your mind and heart!

Take Control of Your Credit & Finances Today with A Simple 3 Step Approach...

There are three major steps that you must complete if you want to totally improve your—and your family's finances. We will discuss them briefly below and go into greater detail of each step later in the book. Be sure you totally grasp the concepts in as effective a manner as possible!

The 3 Step Structured Approach to Improving Your Credit & Finances®

Step 1

BIB N

You can easily remember BIB N

B—stands for Budgeting or Cash Flow Statement

I—stands for Income Statement

B—stands for Balance Sheet

N—stands for Net Worth Statement

The above statements are all personal finance statements, and you will need to create and analyze each one. Be sure to be as accurate as possible with the data you enter.

Once analyzed, you will have to determine ways that you can improve each statement and then come up with a written plan of action for improving each statement so that your financial ratios and net worth will move in the right direction.

Step 2

Remember **NUTTI** or **MUTTI** in your GUTTI to improve your credit score forevermore.

This too, you can also easily remember:

N stands for Negative Information—**M** is for Messed Up--If either occur, your credit will be highly affected as this generally makes up 35% of your credit score.

U stands for Utilization or how you use your credit, and it too is very important as this generally makes up to 30% of your credit score.

T stands for Time and is another important factor as you should keep older accounts open and always pay on time. Just as "i" in time comes before "y" in type, time comes before type when you are memorizing this acronym. Time generally makes up to 15% of your credit score.

T stands for Type and it comes after time. The types of credit you have are important as a good mix is better than no mix. If you have several credit cards, a home loan, and an auto loan that would be a better type of credit than just having several credit cards. The type of credit makes up to 10% of your credit score.

I stands for Inquiries and you should keep your inquiries low if you will be seeking new credit and/or are attempting to improve your credit score. Inquiries also make up to 10% of your credit score.

Note the descending order of the percentages above are:

N or **M** = 35%

U = 30%

T = 15%

T = 10%

I = 10%

Total 100%

Remembering in that order will also help structure the acronym so keep the percentages along with what each acronym represents fresh in your mind.

If your credit is unsatisfactory at this stage, you will have to clean up your credit and work on getting your credit position to an acceptable level so that you can reach your future goals and objectives.

Step 3

My Eyes Tear

My Eyes Tear when I see that my financial future is clear.

The above sentence is a play on words and the memory triggering aspect is:

Your eyes would represent the (**ii's**).

Your tear would represent the (**teeer**) in the following acronym.

The first (**I**) represents your Insurance Planning

The second (**I**) represents your Investment Planning

The (**T**) represents your Tax Planning

The first (**E**) represents your Emergency Fund

The second (**E**) represents your Education Planning

The third (**E**) represents your Estate Planning/Wills

The (**R**) represents your Retirement Planning

You will have to analyze each area of your finances and see what you need to do immediately and, in your future, to improve your position. You should also know at this point what you will need to do in the future as you may not be in financial position now to address all of your financial concerns.

However, you should be aware at this stage of what you need to do in "all areas" of your finances.

Now, do you think you can cultivate a mental framework or mindset that includes the **3 steps above**? Of course you can!

OK, Let's Review

- **BIB N** stands for...

- Remember **NUTTI or MUTTI** in your GUTTI to improve your credit score forevermore and each letter in **NUTTI and MUTTI** stand for...and the percentage in each letter stand for...

- **My EYES TEAR** when I realize my financial future is clear and **your eyes are your (ii's)** and **your tear are your (teeer)** and each letter stands for...

Recite it in your mind until all of the "3 Steps" become second nature to you. Don't get too concerned about the deeper understanding of each letter at this time as they will come to you if you navigate www.realty-1-strategic-advisors.com and/or you purchase **Managing & Improving Your Credit & Finances for this MILLENNIUM**—our new book.

It will all come together for you by navigating **TheWealthIncreaser.com**—our most recent blog site.

With just what you have just learned you put yourself ahead of most consumers when it comes to the effective understanding of personal finance.

This is only the beginning of your journey to financial freedom. Just mastering and understanding the 3 steps listed above are well worth the price you paid for this e-book as you now have the essentials of what you can do in your future to attain lasting success.

Open your mind, ears, and eyes wide as we go into deeper detail of how you utilize **The "3 Step Approach" to Managing & Improving Your Credit & Finances** in your and your family's life—today!

Get your "mindset" to the point where for the rest of your life you will always know:

BIB N—Remember **NUTTI or MUTTI** in your GUTTI to improve your credit score forever more—and my **EYES TEAR** when I realize my financial future is clear.

Once you have the above acronyms solidly memorized you will be well on your way to living your life in a manner that suits you and your family best—not your creditors.

Be sure to comprehend the above acronyms at your highest level. In other words, open your mind, ears, and eyes wide and put on your thinking cap.

In this short book you have the opportunity to master your understanding of credit and finance in a style and manner rarely seen—in personal finance.

This book was intentionally written in a somewhat entertaining and engaging style with serious content that was designed to get your mind to open up.

By reading this short book you should be in great position to apply the information and change your and your family's financial condition for generations.

Final Thoughts

It is critical that you have the proper understanding, and you know how to properly apply the helpful acronyms that you have learned.

You must at all times know:

1)

that you need to properly create and analyze your **B**udget or Cash Flow—so that you know your inflow and outflow of cash on a monthly basis.

Even if you decide to create an **I**ncome Statement, **B**alance Sheet Statement and **N**et Worth Statement later—you need to create at a minimum a Budget or Cash flow Statement—at this time!

2)

Your understanding and application of Remember **NUTTI** or **MUTTI** in your GUTTI to improve your credit score forevermore.

Improving Your Credit Score In A Nutshell

Remember **NUTTI or MUTTI** in your GUTTI to maximize your credit SCORE, FOREVERMORE!

Follow me here...It will make sense...I promise...

N---"Negativity"---try to avoid negative information in your payment history---35% of your score

U---keep "Utilization" and amount owed low---keep debt low---30% of your score

T---always pay on "Time," keep old accounts open---15% of your score

T---keep a good mix and have different "Types" of credit---10% of your score

I---keep "Inquiries" low by loan shopping within a small window---10% of your score

Or Another Way to Look at It

M---don't "Mess up" your credit---try to avoid "negative info" on your report---35%

U---keep "Utilization" at a low percentage of your total debt---keep debt low---30% of your score

T---always pay on "Time," keep old accounts open---15% of your score

T---keep a good mix and "Type" of credit---10% of your score

I---keep "Inquiries" for the last 12 months low if you will be seeking new credit---10% of your score

Did you know that I set you up for a short catchy Acronym (although somewhat strange) that has the potential to help you take control of your credit for the rest of your life?

If you memorize and utilize the following phrase in the right manner, you will be in position to improve your credit position. Feel free to pass it along to your family and friends to help them improve their credit score and credit situation as well.

Although the Acronym (memory trigger) is somewhat "weird" you should easily remember it for the rest of your life by reciting it in your mind on a constant basis—until you are confident that you have it memorized and you understand the underlying concepts behind the acronym.

Remember NUTTI or MUTTI in your GUTTI to maximize your credit SCORE, FOREVERMORE!

By simply memorizing the preceding Acronym—and utilizing the knowledge gained—you can take positive control of your financial situation—and that of your loved ones.

OK—one last time...

N stands for ... and M stands for... 35% of your score

U stands for... and U stands for...30% of your score

T stands for... and T stands for...15% of your score

T stands for... and T stands for...10% of your score

I stands for... and I stands for...10% of your score

OK, your time is up, I'm sure you have all the factors that go into maintaining and improving your credit and credit score mastered.

It is also important that you realize that there are two major scoring models:

1) **FICO score**
2) **VantageScore**

If you utilize the five factors above appropriately you will have a good to excellent credit score regardless of the model that is being used. Always realize that newer models, older models, industry specific models and other models are on the market at the same time and the calculation of your scores will vary depending on the model used by the creditor or the entity requesting your score.

Furthermore, you should know that there are 3 major credit bureaus:

1) **TransUnion**
2) **Equifax**
3) **Experiean**

An easy way to remember the **3 major credit bureaus** is to think that you will be **TEE**ing off—however it won't be for golf—but for improving your credit and credit score!

The above structuring technique brings clarity to help you improve and maintain you credit for the rest of your life. By simply remembering the weird poem or statement—you put yourself in position to always know what you need to do to improve and maintain your credit.

It is also important that you realize that consumers who must concern themselves with the FCRA (Fair Credit Reporting Act) and other corrective credit improvement systems—normally are those who have mismanaged their credit in the past.

It is imperative that you manage and improve your credit and finances in a **more intelligent, consistent, and proactive manner**—in order to avoid getting into a credit position that is adverse for you and your family!

You can choose to learn other creative ways or even learn the FCRA standards and guidelines and other systems of credit and finance management if you choose too—however we do not believe you will find a more effective and efficient system than "Remember **NUTTI or MUTTI** in your GUTTI to improve your credit score forevermore"—that you have learned in this precise and to the point guide.

However, do not use our belief—**as an excuse** to not do your due diligence and determine for yourself if there is a better system or approach that is available that will work better for you and your family.

It is imperative that you use your intelligence to analyze other credit and finance systems in an **analytical, accurate, careful and critical manner** and decide for yourself what works best for you and your family!

If you comprehend and master the use of "Remember **NUTTI or MUTTI** in your GUTTI to improve your credit score forevermore"—you will primarily have what you need—to succeed when it comes to managing and improving your credit for the rest of your life.

It is important that you realize that the **"3 Step Approach"** and the Credit Improvement system mentioned above—will essentially provide you with what you need once you get your credit properly established.

If you desire a comprehensive system that can move you forward on a continuous basis—you have found that with the "3 Step Approach."

Therefore, don't get too uptight or concerned about your credit as long as you have a thorough understanding and you know how to apply in a practical manner (and you actually do so)—"Remember **NUTTI or MUTTI** in your GUTTI to improve your credit score forevermore."

Be sure you understand and remember the **ratio percentages** for each letter as by doing so you will be well ahead of 90% of the population when it comes to the understanding and application of credit. And having the ability to maintain and increase your credit score on a consistent basis is an important skill set that you can pass along to others.

Be sure that you understand that different jargon may be spoken or written regarding the credit factors mentioned above, and it is your responsibility to understand that jargon.

By mastering the **"3 Step Approach"** you will even have a more effective and efficient practical system of credit and finance management and understanding than many professionals who work in the financial industry.

You can choose to waste or perhaps not waste your time by learning about the FCRA (Fair Credit Reporting Act), CFPB (Consumer Finance Protection Bureau), USA.gov—and other credit resources that may add more confusion and frustration than lasting results, or you can choose to know and use "Remember **NUTTI or MUTTI** in your GUTTI to improve your credit score forevermore"—and use the knowledge that you have gained in a manner where you will apply what you have learned to manage and improve your credit in a more stress-free, effective, efficient and results oriented manner!

You can choose to remember that your worthiness, character, capacity, and general reputation plays a major factor in your credit score. It is important that you choose to **"properly focus"** and leave excuses behind—and by comprehending and applying "Remember **NUTTI or MUTTI** in your GUTTI to improve your credit score forevermore" on a consistent basis you can put yourself in position to manage your credit effectively for years to come.

You also should know that by mastering "Remember **NUTTI or MUTTI** in your GUTTI to improve your credit score forevermore"—that does not preclude you from learning additional credit systems and approaches.

However, you must realize that it is truly not necessary for your and your family's future success if you operate in a proactive (gain the knowledge that you need NOW—by using the above acronym in a way that is most beneficial to your credit usage or anticipated credit usage) manner!

It is important that you realize that the amount of credit that is made available to you is often based on the income that you earn in your household and other factors.

It is also important that you realize that your failure to understand how to manage your credit and finances is your choice and you must further realize that you are responsible—not only for your future success but the success of your family and other loved ones as well!

If you have an established and functional **(mental working knowledge)** system of attacking your credit and finances, you can more precisely and more accurately determine what lies ahead (plan better) for you and your family in the financial realm of your and your family's life!

You must live your life purposely and with a real willingness to achieve what you desire!

A **comprehensive system of approaching your credit and finances** leaves nothing to chance—and is an approach that those who truly desire success utilize on a consistent basis!

3)

The final structuring technique in the **"3 Step Approach"** that can help you improve your finances is listed below.

My EYES TEAR

- My eyes tear when I see that my financial picture is clear.
- My eyes tear when I see that my financial independence is near.
- My eyes tear when all my credit card balances disappear.

- My eyes tear when I realize I have no financial fear.
- My eyes tear when I know that I have succeeded this year.

If you were to look at the above poem on the surface it would have some meaning to you. However, the real power of the poem lies beneath the surface—and when properly applied could easily change your mindset or the way that you look at finance in general.

Acronyms can play a key role in simplifying complex problems and can make the mind work easier and eliminate or reduce your stress levels.

In the above poem your **eyes** are your (**ii's**) and your **tears** are your (**teeer**). Let me explain further so that you have a clear understanding.

The above poem is a "play on words." In your financial life you should be concerned with your **i**nsurance and **i**nvestments or another way of looking at it your **eyes** (**ii**).

In your financial life you should also be concerned with your **t**axes, **e**mergency fund, **e**ducation planning, **e**state planning/wills, and **r**etirement planning or another way of looking at it your **tear** (**teeer**).

- By simply remembering the poem above or simply the title of the poem—you bring clarity to your financial understanding immediately.
- By reciting the poem or a line in the poem **daily, weekly, monthly or whatever time frame you prefer** you get to a point where you know all of the areas of your finances that you need to address immediately—thus reducing your stress level—or concern about your finances.
- Used in conjunction with **BIB N**, Remember **NUTTI or MUTTI** in my GUTTI to improve my credit score forevermore—**my eyes tear** when I see that my financial picture is clear has the real effect of **"you knowing all of the areas of your finances that you must address"** at the drop of a hat.
- This alone would greatly reduce the stress in your life and give you a feeling of well-being in your financial realm for the rest of your life—**particularly after you address and improve each area to the maximum effect possible based on your financial condition**—and you can address those areas more appropriately at this time by going to www.realty-1-strategic-advisors.com—NOW—and/or purchasing **Managing & Improving your Credit & Finances for this MILLENNIUM**!
- Although what you have just learned are simple concepts—by reciting and understanding the concepts behind what the acronyms stand for you have immediately

brought clarity to your credit and financial life and that alone would put you well ahead of the general population as far as understanding your credit and finances.

- You have just had the opportunity to master these life-changing acronyms—keep them in the forefront of your mind as you go through life—as by doing so you will improve your and your family's credit and financial future well-being—significantly!

Can you believe that a **"3 Step Approach"** that utilizes **7 words**—has provided the mental framework that allows you to know in a **comprehensive manner—what you need to do for the rest of your life** to manage your credit and finances in a highly effective and efficient manner?

However, don't take the above statement at face value! You must seriously ask yourself—do I have a system that does the above—or do I know of a system that does?

Other Beneficial Structuring Techniques

Another Structuring Technique that can be of great benefit to you and your family that can clarify your finances and reduce your stress levels is to keep your monthly payments from your checking account or check writing to a minimum.

It is simply called **"Keep Your Monthly Bills Under 10—So You Can Win®"**—and it has been very successful at clarifying and simplifying the mental aspect of a person's finances and reducing the financial stress of those who use this structured approach.

Basically, you would have one checking account where you pay your monthly bills from by writing 10 checks or less (or doing 10 debits or less if you prefer online payments) per month. By doing so, your stress level and financial confusion has the potential to be reduced.

For example, you structure your monthly expenses as follows:

- 1) Mortgage Payment
- 2) Electric/ Natural Gas Payment
- 3) Water Payment
- 4) Car Payment
- 5) Cable TV Payment
- 6) Home Phone/Cell Phone Payment
- 7) Internet Payment

- 8) Credit Card 1 Payment
- 9) Credit Card 2 Payment
- 10) Miscellaneous

If you use this strategy—you would also have another separate checking account (debit card) for your other monthly expenses, such as groceries, gas, entertainment, clothing, restaurants, and the like.

By keeping your monthly bills under 10 and having a separate account for— **"all"** of your other monthly expenses, you bring even more structure to your everyday living.

Be sure to keep both accounts properly funded to avoid unnecessary fees and penalties, otherwise this strategy could backfire and actually remove structure—and add to your stress levels.

By writing the 10 bills (or debits) listed above and who knows how many other bills or expenses from the same account monthly "you put the mind in position for confusion—and not clarity."

By keeping your check writing or debiting (under 10—give or take) from a separate account specifically designated for your monthly bills, you immediately put yourself and your family in a better position for future financial success.

If you are now at a point where you mail your bills—it is important that you pay in a timely manner to avoid late fees.

The same is true if you do online bill pay. Also, be sure that you and your online bill pay provider have the most up to date security systems, firewalls, anti-virus, and spyware available—and the latest version of the web browser on the market.

Keep in mind that with a bank—many online bill pay services are free—whereas, if you were to choose Quicken or other online bill pay providers there could be a monthly fee involved.

When it comes to paying your monthly bills, it may be wise for you to have a **"calendar of bills"**—or **"schedule of payments"** that you create for each month of the year to help ensure that you pay all your bills in a timely manner.

In addition, try to be organized with your credit and finances by deciding immediately on whether to save the mail or bill—shred the mail or bill—or trash the mail or bill.

It is important that you have a system of filing—and one that is common is filing from January through December of each year.

It will also help you get your needed information when you file your income taxes. The following is a helpful "monthly payment reminder" that adds clarity to your monthly bill paying and can be posted on your bathroom door, computer or other area that you come into contact with on a daily basis.

January 2023

MONTHLY BILLS	Receive Bill	Payment/Due Date
Water	18th	$70 / 1st
Lowes	19th	$50 / 3rd
Chase Bank	14th	$50 / 3rd
CITI	19th	$100 / 3rd
B of A	22nd	$200 / 4th
Home Mortgage	15th	$1,000 / 10th
Spectrum Cable	30th	$115 / 14th
Golf Fees	27th	$100 / 25th
Gas/Electric	10th	$300 / 10th
Phone/Internet	10th	$95 / 27th
Miscellaneous	10th	$40 / 30th
Student Loan	15th	$140 / 30th

Quarterly: Garbage Fee $50—February—May—August—November

Yearly: Term Life Insurance $500—Payment Due March 1st

Semi-Annual: Auto Insurance—Payment of $300 Due March 1st and September 1st

Note: Life Insurance and Auto Insurance will be paid out of income tax refund

Monthly Tips: GET ALL OF OUR TAX INFORMATION TOGETHER, ASSIGN VALUE TO STUFF THAT WE DONATED TO CHARITIES IN THE PREVIOUS YEAR.

SEE IF WE COULD BENEFIT FROM FLOOD INSURANCE: (WWW.FLOODSMART.ORG)

HOUSEHOLD BASICS—EXCLUDING FOOD:

MORTGAGE/GAS/ELECTRIC/WATER/TRASH = $1,390 MONTHLY

If you have several credit cards with balances, you may want to separate them to add clarity and focus so that you can truly reach your debt payoff goals.

Credit Card Payoff: January 2023

Lowes $50 Balance $800

Chase $50 Balance $925

CITI $100 Balance $4,100

B of A $200 Balance $8,350

Minimum Monthly Payment $400

Total Outstanding Balance $14,175

It is also important that you develop a **"filing system"** for your important documents. Be especially sure to file the following in the appropriate manner:

- Automobile Info
- Adoption Certificate
- Bank Statements
- Birth & Death Certificates
- Car Titles
- Certificate of Marriage
- Contracts
- Deeds
- Estate & Will Documents
- Home Warranties
- Insurance Policies
- Investment Statements
- Manuals
- Medical Records/Information
- Other—anything that you feel is important
- Social Security Card
- Tax Returns
- Written—Audio and Video of Items for Insurer—be sure to file at separate locations
- Also, consider scanning your important documents to a CD—and file at separate locations

Be sure to make "credit card payoff isolation and filing system" a part of your mindset—or thought process on a consistent or as-needed basis.

Doing so will help ensure future success in your credit and financial life!

You are now on a credit and financial journey where— "you" can do the driving in a manner where you can avoid potholes and accidents that so many other consumers are unable to avoid!

Major improvement in the management of your credit and finances can now happen for you and your family!

You are now aware of empowering structuring techniques that include:

- The "**3 Step Structured Approach to Improving Your Credit & Finances®"**
- **"Keep Your Monthly Bills under 10—So You Can Win"**
- **"Calendar of Bills" or "Schedule of Bills"**
- **"Calendar of Bills" for Credit Card Payoff**
- **"Filing System"**

Now that you have a conceptual understanding of several structuring techniques you are well on your way to success and living your life on your terms.

It is important that you understand all the concepts related to the structuring techniques that have been discussed. Your future financial and life success will depend in large part on your ability to properly understand and apply the structuring techniques that you have learned in this book.

BONUS SECTION

100 Money Saving Strategies

We recommend that you increase your income and pay your debt off in the most efficient manner possible!

However, we realize that in some cases that is not always possible, depending on the current economic environment.

Therefore, we provide a list of cost saving measures that you may be able to take to improve your monthly cash flow position.

AUTOMOBILE

- Purchase a used car instead of a new one

- Always negotiate based on price when purchasing a car—never payments.
- Get your loan up front prior to going to dealership.
- Consider the total cost of ownership when you purchase a car.
- Thoroughly research the vehicle you are considering purchasing.
- Eliminate all dealer add-on fees other than those that are truly necessary.
- Consider a private car seller—if you are in a strong cash position.
- Always do a thorough inspection when buying a used car.
- Run the numbers to see if leasing a vehicle is more advantageous to you than buying.
- Negotiate the value of your trade-in before you negotiate for the new car.
- Keep your car in good running condition by doing regular maintenance.
- Consider carpooling.
- Use the right octane (gas) for your vehicle.

ELECTRONICS

- Consider a cell phone instead of a landline.
- Get the best cell phone deal possible based on your usage.
- Shop around for the best software and internet rates.

FINANCIAL

- Get the best cell phone deal possible based on your usage.
- Shop around for the best software and internet rates.
- Consider a credit union rather than a bank to avoid/reduce fees.
- Use only your banks ATM.
- Ask your credit card company for a reduction in your interest rate.
- Consider direct deposit and online bill pay.
- Be sure to enroll in your companies 401k or other retirement account—particularly if there is an employer match.
- Buy no-load or low load mutual funds

CREDIT

- Eliminate your expensive annual fee Airline Credit Card
- Lower your credit card interest if you have excellent credit
- Avoid bounced checks and costly overdraft charges
- Set up bank alerts to avoid fraud and other fees
- Sign up for automatic federal student loan payments
- Refinance your home at a lower rate with a good lender by going to quickenloans.com and lendingtree.com
- Consider a cell phone instead of a landline.
- Get the best cell phone deal possible based on your usage.
- Shop around for the best software and internet rates.
- Consider a credit union rather than a bank to avoid/reduce fees.

· Use only your banks ATM.
· Ask your credit card company for a reduction in your interest rate.
· Consider direct deposit and online bill pay.

INSURANCE

· Consider and insurer that offers multiple car and home discounts, defensive driving, security and other discounts on home and auto policies.
· Buy term life insurance and invest the difference in savings from whole life.
· Shop your insurance coverage and be sure you are dealing with a highly rated and solvent company.
· Drop comprehensive insurance if your vehicle is not worth that much.
· Try to eliminate your PMI (private mortgage insurance) or MIP (mortgage insurance premium) as soon as possible.
· Avoid specialty insurers—when possible.
· Choose the best health coverage for you and your family.

MISCELLANEOUS

· Do small repairs around the house yourself. Consider budget or levelized billing—with your utility providers—will also help you plan your future more effectively.
· Make your own baby food.
· Take lunch to work.
· Buy in bulk when possible.
· Do comparison shopping appropriately by considering unit pricing and generics.
· Grow some of your own food/eat healthy.
· Travel in the off season and shop around for the best airline and hotel deals.
· Consider bread and breakfast instead of a hotel.
· Use coupons when you eat out.
· Use the library more.
· Avoid newspaper and magazine subscriptions that you rarely read.
· Use your "imaginative spirit" to find other areas where you can save.
· Lower your entertainment costs by going to fansnap.com
· Unsubscribe from deal e-mails.
· Improve your fuel economy
· Use a car buying service to get a great deal
· Spot lower prices shopping online
· Rent designer clothing instead of buying at renttherunway.com
· Scan barcodes when you are shopping to compare prices with other retailers and online stores—when necessary.
· Listen to free audio books at ambling books, librivox, and project gutenburg. You can also try your local library.
· Eliminate your landline phone if you can do so effectively
· Text for free by downloading the app—if you are a heavy text messenger

· Eliminate fees on treasury investments by purchasing directly from www.treasurydirect.gov—by doing so you will avoid brokerage commissions, management fees and possible sales loads in mutual funds.
· Slash expenses with ETF's
· Avoid taxes on bonds by purchasing municipal bonds
· Cut your drug costs by considering generics
· Raise your insurance deductibles
· Look for lower life insurance rates by going to accuquote.com or lifequotes.com—you will need to take a basic medical exam before getting the final rate

REAL ESTATE

If you are considering purchasing a home or refinancing—you can go to www.**quickenloans.com** or www.**lendingtree.com** along with local mortgage lenders in your area—to determine what loan will best suit you—and your family. You can compare closing costs, APR's and Par rates to determine what loan will best serve your—and your family's long-term interests.
· Purchase, refinance or sell your home at the right time.
· Always have your home inspected prior to purchase or sale.
· Negotiate your rental payment if you are a renter.
· Get a free energy audit for your home.
· Change your filters and make energy improvements in your home, wherever possible.
· Water your yard and plants early—rather than later to avoid evaporation.
· Dress appropriately for the season, and adjust thermostat in your home accordingly.

SHOPPING

• Haggle like an expert (download free applications on your smartphone) with shopping applications at shoppingbythefind, retailmenot, pricegrabber, pounce, poachit, goodzer, favado, google shopper, redlaser or shopsavvy.
· Scan barcodes when you are shopping to compare prices with other retailers and online stores—when necessary.
· Take inventory of where you are spending your money and make cut backs where you can.
· See if you really need an extended warranty.
· Use intelligence in your shopping patterns—such as buying after the holiday— buying at end of the season etcetera.
· Set up a monthly budget—and stick to it—so that you can reach your goals—get family involved.
· Purchase with cash or debit card whenever possible.
· Stop the use of your credit card.
· Don't shop while you are hungry or tired.
· Use your rebates if you purchase a product that offers rebates.
· Don't pay for fancy extras that you don't use or need.
· Have a garage sale—will also help de-clutter your house.

· Workout at home or in neighborhood—either temporarily or permanently.
· Change to fluorescent, halogen incandescent, light-emitting diode or LED—light bulbs.
· Install a water saving showerhead
· Conserve energy on your electronics by purchasing a Belkin Conserve Smart AV ($29 at Amazon.com) · Install a programmable thermostat

On the following pages the **3 Step Approach** is presented from a different perspective so you can learn the system more efficiently.

It is important that you know the importance of being exposed to the right financial management systems at the right time...

In life we all have unique environments, exposures, experiences and the way that we pursue excellence, and it is important that we learn all that we can from those factors so that we can direct our future actions in a manner that is more beneficial for ourselves and those whom we come into contact with.

It is imperative that you know the importance of why you must be **exposed to financial systems** in general, and **exposed to financial systems** that you can readily learn and apply in your daily life to be more specific—that will truly take you towards your goals that are most significant and meaningful to you and your family, in a very efficient manner.

We all want to do things that bring us joy, however from time to time we must dive into topics that are uncomfortable. For many, personal finance or the management of their finances can be a burdensome or uncomfortable process, however it no longer has to be!

By gaining the right financial knowledge you can cover all of your bases and have a comprehensive approach in the management of your finances that can lead to you building wealth more effectively at the **various stages in your life** so that you can do more of what brings joy into your life.

What you need to know financially

You need to know just what does personal finance entail and how broad or wide a net you must cast, as most people have no idea of the magnitude- or lack thereof—of financial planning in an all-encompassing way. At a basic level and for starters you need to know your monthly intake and outflow of cash, as that is what all of the other areas of your finances will be based on and will flow from.

In easy-to-understand format, you must know how to:

1) Utilize personal finance statements appropriately

1. Establish a personal **b**udget or cash flow statement at a minimum

2. Create a personal **i**ncome statement
3. Create a personal **b**alance sheet
4. Create a personal **n**et worth statement

2) Gain mastery of how you manage your credit

Negative information must be kept off of your credit report

Utilization of your available credit must be at a reasonable level

Time of open accounts is important

Type of accounts are important

Inquiries must be kept at a reasonable level

3) Comprehensively understand your finances in the following areas

Insurance

Investments

Taxes

Emergency fund

Education planning

Estate Planning/Wills

Retirement planning

By just being **exposed to** the **3 steps** above--you are far ahead of the average consumer who for the most part has no real understanding of what personal finance encompasses--let alone the ability to use the knowledge of what personal finance encompasses to their and their family's greater benefit.

What you need to do financially

Now that you have knowledge of what you need to know (pun intended) **you must take the right steps** and put into action the results of your cash flow statement or budget at a minimum. Whether you have a monthly surplus or a monthly deficit you are now in position for more effective planning from this point forward.

If you are comfortable with numbers, you may also want to create an income statement and balance sheet so that you can determine your net worth at this time--and improve upon your net worth in the coming years.

The creation of a "properly funded emergency fund" will go a long way in helping you increase your net worth in future years!

You must also gain mastery over how you manage your credit by knowing how to **utilize your knowledge of the 5 credit factors**—as that knowledge can prevent you from getting into a difficult financial hole where climbing out is difficult or highly unlikely (you may need to consider filing bankruptcy as a real option).

Finally, you must know how to select the appropriate insurance products and investment options along with doing, education planning, estate planning and retirement planning in a manner that is more advantageous for you and your family—not creditors or others who have no real concern for your lasting success.

The importance of reviewing what you do financially

Now that you have a comprehensive overview of your finances and you have been **exposed** to all that you need to know (and do) to work toward making your wealth building goals come true, you "must" be aware of your need to review!

You must review your personal finance statements, including your emergency fund to make sure you are adequately protected. You must review your understanding of the 5 credit factors so that you can make the right or at a minimum, good decisions as it relates to your use of credit.

You must review your insurance, investments, taxes, education planning, estate planning/wills, and retirement planning on a routine basis to see where improvements can be made.

Regardless of your past experiences, the environment in which you grew up in and the positive or negative exposures in your life, you are now in position to change all of that to your advantage—and by being **exposed to personal finance** in a way that you can readily understand and utilize, you are now ready to take your prize.

It is important that you are **exposed to all areas of financial planning** that you need to do throughout your life at the earliest time possible. By doing so you can get out in front of potential disruptions and "proactively plan your future" in a manner that is more advantageous for you and your family.

You can put yourself in position where you can live with confidence and the success that you desire will not only occur—it will be expected. You no longer need to approach your financial future with doubt, uncertainty, and a feeling of "can't do"—as by purchasing this book you have positioned yourself in a major way to make your dreams come true.

All the best because of your willingness to be "exposed to financial systems" that can lead to lasting success.

Thanks for purchasing **The 3 Step Structured Approach to Managing Your Credit & Finances**

Go out and truly attain all your wealth building and life goals...

ISBN: 978-1-953994-02-8

Made in the USA
Monee, IL
08 November 2026

67994721R00017